Our Favorite Blueberry Recipes

An imprint of
The Globe Pequot Publishing Group, Inc., Essex, CT

Keep pancakes warm and yummy. Just arrange them on a baking sheet, set in a 200-degree oven, then serve as needed.

Blueberry Buttermilk Pancakes

Serves 4

1-1/2 c. all-purpose flour
1/2 c. whole-wheat flour
1/4 c. sugar
2-1/4 t. baking powder
1/2 t. baking soda
1/2 t. salt
2 eggs, beaten
1 t. vanilla extract
2 c. buttermilk
1/4 c. butter, melted
1 c. fresh or frozen blueberries
Garnish: maple syrup, extra blueberries

In a large bowl, mix together flours, sugar, baking powder, baking soda and salt; set aside. In a separate bowl, beat together eggs, vanilla, buttermilk and melted butter. Add egg mixture to flour mixture; stir together until a lumpy batter forms. Do not overmix. Spoon batter by 1/3 cupfuls into a buttered skillet over medium heat; sprinkle each with blueberries. Cook for 2 to 3 minutes on each side, until golden and cooked through. Serve with a drizzle of maple syrup and a few extra blueberries, as desired.

Serve up an old-fashioned fruit salad at breakfast...it's easy! Toss together ripe summer fruits like blueberries, strawberries, orange and kiwi slices. Drizzle with a dressing made by whisking together 1/2 cup honey, 1/4 cup lime juice and one teaspoon lime zest.

Baked Blueberry-Almond Oatmeal

Makes 9 servings

2 eggs, beaten
1-1/2 c. milk
1/4 c. brown sugar, packed
1/4 c. butter, melted
1-1/2 t. baking powder
3 c. rolled oats, uncooked
1 t. cinnamon
1 t. almond or vanilla extract
1/4 t. salt
1/3 c. sliced almonds
1 c. fresh or frozen blueberries

Stir all ingredients together in a large bowl. Spoon batter into a greased 8"x8" glass baking pan. Bake at 350 degrees for 30 to 35 minutes; cut into squares and serve.

A jar of honey is a sweet addition to the breakfast table to enjoy on hot toast, pancakes or drizzle into hot tea. If the honey has crystallized, simply set the jar in a pan of hot water. After a few minutes, it will be ready to use again.

Apple & Berry Breakfast Crisp

Makes 9 servings

4 apples, peeled, cored and thinly sliced
1-1/2 c. blueberries
3 T. frozen orange juice concentrate, thawed
2 T. brown sugar, packed
2 T. all-purpose flour
1 t. cinnamon
Optional: vanilla yogurt

Combine all ingredients except optional yogurt in a large bowl; stir until fruit is evenly coated. Spoon into a lightly greased 8"x8" baking pan. Sprinkle Oat Topping evenly over fruit. Bake, uncovered, at 350 degrees for 30 to 35 minutes, until apples are tender. Serve warm with yogurt, if desired.

Oat Topping:

1/2 c. quick-cooking oats
3 T. brown sugar, packed
3 T. butter, melted
1 T. all-purpose flour

Combine all ingredients; mix well.

Let everyone choose their favorite juice for breakfast. Fill old-fashioned glass milk bottles with a variety of juices, and then tuck them in a wire milk bottle carrier...so easy to pass around the table!

Blueberry Breakfast Cake

Serves 6 to 8

2 c. blueberries
1-1/2 c. plus 2 T. all-purpose flour, divided
1 t. baking powder
1/2 t. salt
1/2 c. butter
1 c. sugar
2 eggs
1/3 c. milk
1 t. vanilla extract
Garnish: sugar

Toss blueberries in 2 tablespoons flour; set aside. Sift together remaining flour, baking powder and salt; set aside. Cream butter and sugar together until light and fluffy; add eggs, one at a time, beating well. Add flour mixture to creamed mixture alternately with milk. Mix for 5 minutes. Stir in vanilla and floured blueberries. Pour into a well-greased 8"x8" baking pan. Sprinkle top with sugar. Bake at 350 degrees for 35 to 40 minutes.

Make some yogurt pops for kids on the go. Insert wooden treat sticks through the tops of a pack of individual yogurts and freeze overnight.

Breakfast Milkshake

Makes 2 servings

2 ripe bananas, sliced into 1-inch chunks
1/4 c. blueberries
5 to 10 whole strawberries, quartered and hulled
1/2 c. milk

Combine fruits in a plastic freezer bag; seal and freeze for 3 hours to overnight. Place the frozen fruits in a blender or food processor. If fruits are rock-hard, let them thaw a little. Add milk and process until smooth and thick. Pour into mugs and serve with spoons.

Get the day off to a great start! Put together a make-ahead breakfast casserole and refrigerate. The next day, pop it in the oven for a hot, hearty breakfast with no fuss at all.

Blueberry Breakfast Casserole

Makes 6 servings

8 slices bread, torn into pieces
8-oz. pkg. cream cheese, sliced
1 c. fresh blueberries
8 eggs, beaten
1-1/2 c. milk
Garnish: pancake syrup

Spread bread pieces evenly in a greased 13"x9" baking pan. Arrange cream cheese slices over bread. Sprinkle with blueberries; set aside. In a large bowl, beat together eggs and milk; pour over top. Cover and refrigerate overnight. The next morning, cover with aluminum foil and bake at 350 degrees for 30 minutes. Remove foil; bake for 30 minutes more. Serve with pancake syrup.

Invite friends over for brunch before a day of shopping...
a terrific way to start the day!

Light Blueberry Danish

Makes 4 servings

8-oz. tube refrigerated reduced-fat crescent dinner rolls
1/2 c. Neufchâtel or light cream cheese, softened
2 T. sugar or powdered sweetener
1/2 c. fresh blueberries

Unroll dough into 4 rectangles; firmly press perforations together to seal. In a bowl, blend cheese and sugar; spread onto dough rectangles to within 1/2 inch of edges. Top evenly with blueberries. Bring opposite corners of rectangles together; press together to seal. Place on an ungreased baking sheet. Bake at 375 degrees for 15 to 18 minutes, until golden.

For a scrumptious pancake and waffle topping, combine 1/2 cup fresh blueberries, 1/2 cup softened butter and one tablespoon honey in a blender. Process until smooth. Yum!

Yummy Blueberry Waffles

Makes 4 waffles, serves 4

2 eggs
2 c. all-purpose flour
1-3/4 c. milk
1/2 c. oil
1 T. sugar
4 t. baking powder
1/4 t. salt
1/2 t. vanilla extract
1-1/2 c. blueberries

In a large bowl, beat eggs with an electric mixer on medium speed until fluffy. Add remaining ingredients except berries; beat just until smooth. Spray a waffle iron with non-stick vegetable spray. Pour batter by 1/2 cupfuls onto the preheated waffle iron. Scatter berries over batter. Bake according to manufacturer's directions, until golden.

Day-old bread is excellent for making French toast and breakfast stratas. It keeps its texture better than very fresh bread...it's thrifty too!

Blueberry French Toast

Serves 6

2 c. fresh or frozen blueberries
2 T. cornstarch
1/4 c. sugar
1/2 c. orange juice
1/2 c. plus 3 T. water, divided
3 eggs, beaten
6 slices bread
2 T. butter, melted
cinnamon-sugar to taste

Spread blueberries in a greased 13"x9" baking pan; set aside. In a bowl, combine cornstarch, sugar, orange juice and 1/2 cup water; pour over blueberries. In a shallow bowl, whisk together eggs and remaining water. Dip bread slices into egg mixture; arrange over blueberries in pan. Brush bread slices with butter and sprinkle with cinnamon-sugar. Bake, uncovered, at 350 degrees for 15 to 20 minutes, until bread is lightly toasted and sauce is bubbly and thickened. Serve toast slices topped with blueberry mixture from pan.

A well-loved china teapot that's been handed down to you makes a sweet vase for daisies, bachelor buttons and zinnia from the farmers' market.

Blueberry-Lemon Crepes

Makes 6 servings

3-oz. pkg. cream cheese, softened
1-1/2 c. half-and-half
1 T. lemon juice
3.4-oz. pkg. instant lemon pudding mix
1/2 c. biscuit baking mix
1 egg
6 T. milk
1 c. blueberry pie filling

Combine cream cheese, half-and-half, lemon juice and dry pudding mix in a bowl. Beat with an electric mixer on low speed for 2 minutes. Refrigerate for 30 minutes. Lightly grease a 6" skillet and place over medium-high heat. In a bowl, combine biscuit baking mix, egg and milk. Beat until smooth. Pour 2 tablespoons of batter into skillet for each crepe. Rotating the skillet quickly, allow batter to cover the bottom of the skillet. Cook each crepe until lightly golden, then flip, cooking again until just golden. Spoon 2 tablespoonfuls of cream cheese mixture onto each crepe and roll up. Top with remaining cream cheese mixture and pie filling.

A neighborly gesture never goes out of style. Wrap homemade muffins or scones in a tea towel, tuck them into a basket with a jar of jam and deliver to a friend. A sweet gift that says "I'm thinking of you!"

Barbara's Best Blueberry Buns

Makes 16

13-oz. tube refrigerated cinnamon rolls
1 c. frozen blueberries, thawed and well drained
1/2 c. blueberry preserves
1 t. lemon zest
1/3 c. chopped pecans
small amount milk

Split cinnamon rolls in half horizontally; set aside icing. Spray 16 muffin cups with non-stick vegetable spray. Press each roll piece into the bottom of a muffin cup, about 1/2-inch thick. In a bowl, mix blueberries, preserves and lemon zest. Evenly spoon into cups; top with pecans. Bake at 350 degrees for 10 to 12 minutes, until golden. Cool for 5 minutes; turn out of muffin cups. Thin icing with a few drops of milk; drizzle over buns. Serve warm.

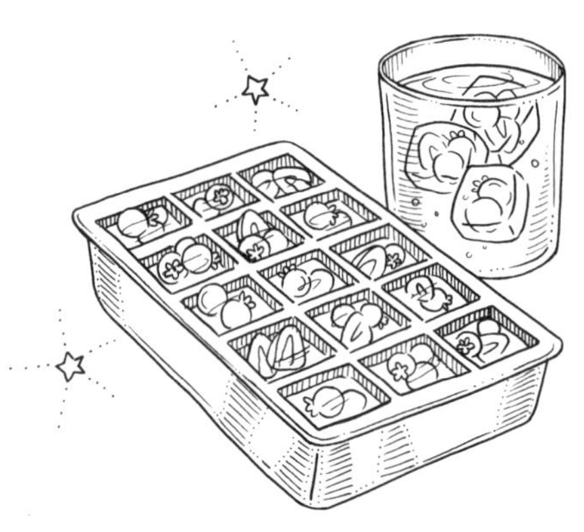

Freeze strawberry slices or blueberries in ice cube trays...
toss several cubes into glasses of orange juice right before serving.

Good Morning Blueberry Shake

Makes 4 servings

2-1/2 c. blueberries
1-1/4 c. apple juice
1 c. frozen vanilla yogurt
1/4 c. milk
3/4 t. cinnamon
Garnish: additional blueberries

Combine all ingredients except garnish in a blender and process until smooth. Garnish with additional blueberries. Serve immediately.

A big square of red-checked homespun fabric makes a cozy liner for a basket of freshly baked muffins or scones. No hemming needed...just pull away the threads to create a fringe.

Lemon Blueberry Scones

Makes 8 scones

2 c. all-purpose flour
1/3 c. sugar
2 t. baking powder
1/2 t. baking soda
1/4 t. salt
1 t. lemon zest
1 c. lemon yogurt
1 egg, beaten
1/4 c. butter, melted
1 c. fresh or frozen blueberries

In a large bowl, combine flour, sugar, baking powder, baking soda, salt and lemon zest; mix well and set aside. In another bowl, combine yogurt, egg and butter; stir into flour mixture just until moistened. Fold in blueberries. Drop batter onto a greased baking sheet by heaping tablespoonfuls, 2 inches apart. Bake at 400 degrees for 15 to 18 minutes, until lightly golden. Drizzle Glaze over warm scones.

Glaze:

1/2 c. powdered sugar
1 T. lemon juice
1/2 t. lemon zest

Stir together ingredients to a drizzling consistency.

Enjoy the fun of the diner at home! Include a napkin dispenser, sugar shaker, salt & pepper, creamer, red and yellow squirt bottles and, of course, a menu with today's special!

Patriotic Bread

Makes 8 servings

3 c. all-purpose flour
1 t. baking soda
1 t. baking powder
1 t. salt
1 c. sugar
1/2 c. butter, softened
2 eggs
1 c. buttermilk
1 c. whole-berry cranberry sauce
1 c. blueberries

Combine flour, baking soda, baking powder and salt; set aside. Cream sugar and butter together in a large mixing bowl; blend in eggs and buttermilk. Add flour mixture; mix well. Stir in cranberry sauce and blueberries; pour into a greased 9"x5" loaf pan. Bake at 375 degrees for one hour and 10 minutes or until a toothpick inserted in the center comes out clean. Remove from pan; cool on a wire rack.

A good laugh is sunshine in the house.

-Thackeray

Blueberry Bread

Makes one loaf

1 c. sugar
3 c. plus 2 t. all-purpose flour, divided
1 t. salt
4 t. baking powder
1 egg, beaten
1 c. milk
2 T. butter, melted
juice of 1/2 lemon
1 c. blueberries

Sift together sugar, 3 cups of flour, salt and baking powder in a bowl. Add egg, milk and butter. Mix with a wooden spoon, do not beat. Add lemon juice. Toss blueberries with remaining flour, fold into mixture. Spread in a greased 9"x5" loaf pan and bake at 350 degrees for one hour.

Baker's secret! Grease muffin cups on the bottoms and just halfway up the sides. Muffins will bake up nicely puffed on top.

Julie's Quick Blueberry-Banana Muffins

Makes 1-1/2 dozen

15-1/4 oz. pkg. butter yellow cake mix
1 t. baking powder
2 ripe bananas, mashed
3 eggs, beaten
2/3 c. oil
1/3 c. water
1 c. fresh blueberries, divided

Mix together dry cake mix and baking powder in a large bowl; set aside. In another bowl, mix together bananas, eggs, oil, water and 2/3 cup blueberries. Add banana mixture to cake mixture; stir until moistened. Scoop batter into paper-lined muffin cups by 1/2 cupfuls. Top each muffin with a few remaining blueberries, gently pushing berries halfway into batter. Bake at 375 degrees for 15 to 17 minutes. Remove muffins to a wire rack; allow to cool for 15 minutes and serve.

Use an old-fashioned ice cream scoop to fill muffin cups with batter...no drips, no spills and muffins turn out perfectly sized.

Berry Sunrise Muffins

Makes one dozen

1/2 c. sugar
1/4 c. butter, melted
2 T. orange juice
1 egg, beaten
2 c. all-purpose flour
2 t. baking powder
1/2 t. salt
2/3 c. almond milk or dairy milk
1/2 c. fresh blueberries
1/2 c. fresh strawberries, hulled and chopped

In a bowl, blend together sugar, melted butter and orange juice. Add egg; beat until combined. Slowly stir in flour, baking powder and salt. Add milk; stir until just combined. Fold in berries. Fill 12 greased or paper-lined muffin tins 2/3 full of batter; sprinkle with Topping. Bake at 400 degrees for about 20 minutes, until lightly golden and a toothpick tests done.

Topping:

1/4 c. all-purpose flour
1/4 c. sugar
1 T. butter
1/8 t. cinnamon

In a small bowl, mix ingredients with a fork until crumbly.

Molded gelatin salads were everywhere in the 1950's! Vintage molds can be found at flea markets...dress up a kitchen wall with a whimsical display.

Blueberry Butter

Makes 4 pints

3 pts. blueberries
4 c. apples, peeled, cored and coarsely chopped
4 c. sugar
1/2 t. cinnamon
1/8 t. mace
1/8 t. allspice
1/8 t. nutmeg

Combine ingredients in a heavy saucepan; heat over low heat until sugar dissolves, stirring often. Increase heat to medium-high; bring to a boil, stirring constantly. Reduce heat to low; continue simmering until mixture is thick, about 45 to 50 minutes, stirring often. Divide and pour into four, one-pint jars. Cover and keep refrigerated up to 2 weeks.

Instant ice cream social! Alongside pints of ice cream, set out toppings like sliced bananas, peanuts, hot fudge sauce and whipped cream. Berry Dessert Topping would be yummy, too!

Berry Dessert Topping

Makes 6 servings

6 c. frozen blackberries, blueberries, raspberries and strawberries, partially thawed and divided

1 c. sugar

3 T. cornstarch

1/2 c. water

Mash one cup berries in a large saucepan; set aside. Mix together sugar and cornstarch in a small bowl. Add sugar mixture and water to mashed berries; stir until combined. Cook and stir over medium heat until mixture boils and thickens. Boil one minute longer; remove from heat. Cool to lukewarm; stir in remaining whole berries. Cool completely before serving.

Sharing Mom's and Grandma's tried & true canning recipes is a great way to hand down favorite recipes that generations have loved. Keep the recipes, but be sure to update the preserving methods if needed. Some ways Grandma canned, using a wax seal or the inversion method for jams & jellies, are no longer a good way to keep foods their freshest.

Spiced Blueberry Jam

Makes 8 1/2-pint jars

4-1/2 c. fresh blueberries, crushed
1/2 t. cinnamon
1/2 t. ground cloves
7 c. sugar
juice of 1 lemon
3-oz. pkg. liquid fruit pectin
8 1/2-pint canning jars and lids, sterilized

Combine blueberries, spices, sugar and lemon juice in a large stockpot. Bring to a boil over medium-high heat, stirring constantly. Boil for 2 minutes; add pectin. Boil again, stirring constantly, for one minute longer. Remove from heat; skim off foam. Spoon into hot sterilized jars, leaving 1/4-inch headspace. Wipe rims; secure with lids and rings. Process in a boiling water bath for 10 minutes. Set jars on a towel to cool completely; check for seals.

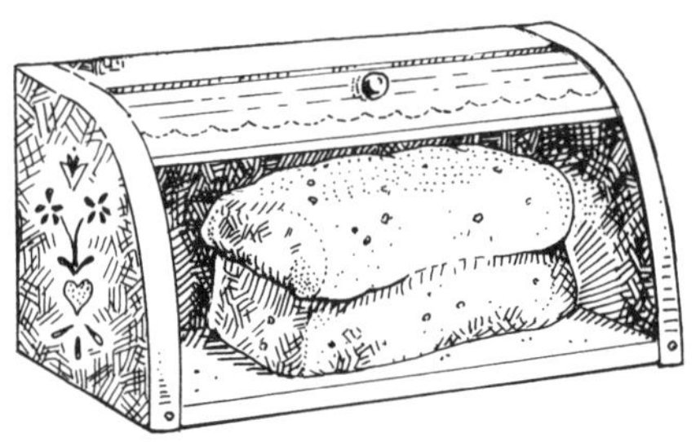

Want to try making your favorite conventional bread recipe using a bread machine? It's simple. If the recipe makes 2 loaves, just divide all the ingredients in half to produce one bread-machine loaf. Don't divide the amount of yeast, though...it should still be about 2 teaspoons.

Blueberry Freezer Jam

Makes 7 containers

6 c. blueberries, crushed
5 c. sugar
2 T. lemon juice
3/4 c. water
1-3/4 oz. pkg. powdered pectin
7 1/2-pint freezer-safe plastic containers and lids, sterilized

Combine berries, sugar and lemon juice in a bowl; let stand for 10 minutes. In a small saucepan over medium-high heat, bring water and pectin to a boil. Cook and stir for one minute. Add to berry mixture; stir for 3 minutes. Ladle into freezer containers; cool to room temperature. Cover and let stand overnight at room temperature before freezing. May be frozen up to one year. Keep refrigerated up to 3 weeks after opening.

Enjoy fresh blueberries year 'round...just freeze them during berry season! Spread ripe berries in a single layer on a baking sheet and freeze until solid, then store them in plastic freezer bags. Later, pour out just the amount you need.

Luscious Blueberry Syrup

Makes about 2-1/2 cups

1/2 c. sugar
1 T. cornstarch
1/3 c. water
2 c. fresh or frozen blueberries

In a saucepan over medium heat, combine sugar and cornstarch. Stir in water gradually. Add berries; bring to a boil. Boil, stirring constantly, for one minute, or until mixture thickens. Serve warm, or pour into a covered jar and keep in the refrigerator for several days.

Buttery cinnamon toast warms you right up on a chilly morning, and it's ready in a jiffy. Spread softened butter generously on one side of toasted bread and sprinkle with cinnamon-sugar. Broil for one to 2 minutes, until hot and bubbly.

Cinnamon-Blueberry Sauce

Serves 4

1/4 c. brown sugar substitute
2 t. cornstarch
2 c. frozen blueberries
1/4 c. water
2 T. lemon or lime juice
2 t. cinnamon

Combine brown sugar substitute and cornstarch in a small saucepan. Add blueberries, water, lemon or lime juice and cinnamon. Bring to a boil over medium heat. Reduce heat and simmer, uncovered, for 5 minutes, stirring frequently.

People are always good company when they are doing what they really enjoy.

–Samuel Butler

Blueberry Salsa

Makes 8 servings

3 c. blueberries, divided
1/2 c. red pepper, diced
1/2 c. red onion, diced
zest and juice of 1 lemon
1/2 c. fresh cilantro, chopped
coarse salt and pepper to taste
Optional: favorite corn chips

Set aside one cup whole blueberries in a bowl; chop remaining berries and add to bowl. Add remaining ingredients, except for corn chips; mix gently. Cover and refrigerate for at least 30 minutes to blend the flavors. Serve with corn chips, if desired.

Toasted oats can take the place of chopped nuts in cakes and cookies, adding crunch and nutty flavor. Simply cook uncooked oats in a little butter until golden. Cool before adding to a recipe.

Blueberry Nut Crunch

Makes 10 servings

15-1/4 oz. pkg. yellow cake mix
6 T. all-purpose flour
1 pt. blueberries
20-oz. can crushed pineapple, drained
3/4 c. butter, melted
1/2 c. chopped nuts

Prepare cake mix according to package directions; stir in flour. Mix blueberries and pineapple into batter; spread in a greased 13"x9" baking pan. Drizzle with melted butter; sprinkle with nuts. Bake at 350 degrees for one hour. Cut into squares to serve.

For best results when baking, let butter stand at room temperature at least 30 minutes before using. Short on time? Speed things up by grating chilled sticks of butter with a cheese grater.

Chocolate Blueberry Snack Cake *Makes 9 to 12 servings*

1 c. boiling water
1 t. baking soda
1 c. all-purpose flour
1 c. sugar
1/4 c. baking cocoa
1/4 c. butter, sliced
2 T. brewed coffee, cooled
1 egg, beaten
1/2 c. fresh blueberries
Garnish: powdered sugar

Combine boiling water and baking soda in a cup; set aside. In a large bowl, combine flour, sugar and baking cocoa; mix well. Add butter and baking soda mixture; stir until butter is melted. Add coffee and egg; mix well. Fold in blueberries. Pour batter into a greased 8"x8" glass baking pan. Bake at 350 degrees for 30 to 35 minutes, until cake tests done. Sprinkle with powdered sugar while still warm; cut into squares.

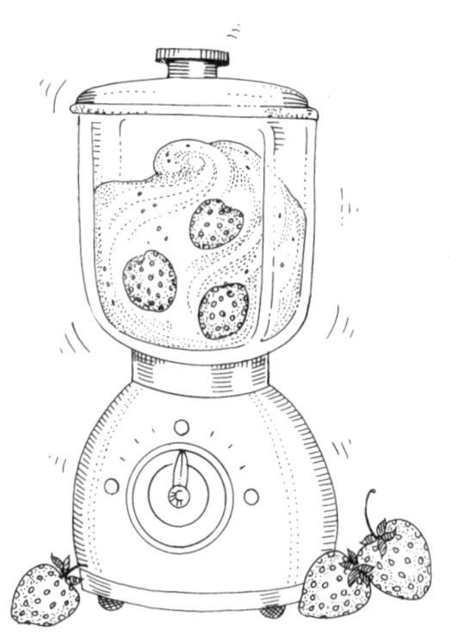

Using frozen fruit in smoothies will make them icy-cold without adding extra water from ice cubes.

Perfect Purple Smoothie

Makes 2 servings

1-1/2 c. frozen mixed fruit
1-1/4 c. frozen blueberries
1 to 1-1/2 c. orange juice
1/2 c. milk
1/4 c. rolled oats, uncooked
1/2 c. vanilla Greek yogurt or regular yogurt
6 ice cubes

Combine all ingredients into a blender. Blend very well until oats are thoroughly mixed in. Serve in tall glasses.

Hang an old-fashioned peg rack inside the back door...
you'll always know where to find your car keys,
the kids' backpacks and the dog's leash!

Blueberry Flaxseed Smoothies

Serves 4

1 banana, cut into chunks
1/2 c. blueberries
1 c. low-fat vanilla yogurt
1 c. fat-free milk
2 T. ground flaxseed
Garnish: fresh strawberries, blueberries, flaxseed

Combine all ingredients except garnish in a blender; process on high setting until smooth. Pour into glasses. Garnish with fruit and flaxseed.

Use empty tin cans with bright veggie labels to hold simple bouquets of black-eyed susans, zinnias, daisies and other cut flowers. Line them up along the center of your table...charming!

Minty Melon Salad

Serves 10

1 c. water
3/4 c. sugar
3 T. lime juice
1-1/2 t. fresh mint, chopped
5 c. watermelon, cubed
3 c. cantaloupe, cubed
3 c. honeydew, cubed
2 c. nectarines, pitted and sliced
1 c. blueberries
Garnish: fresh mint sprigs

Combine water, sugar, lime juice and mint in a saucepan; bring to a boil. Boil for 2 minutes, stirring constantly. Remove from heat; cover and cool completely. Combine all fruit in a large bowl. Pour cooled dressing over fruit; stir until well coated. Cover and chill for at least 2 hours, stirring occasionally. Drain liquid before serving. Garnish with fresh mint sprigs.

Write or paste your most-used recipes on index cards...they'll fit perfectly into a flip photo album. You'll easily find the recipe you want, and the plastic pages will protect recipes from spatters.

Easy Berry Salad

Serves 4 to 6

1 c. fresh strawberries, hulled and halved or quartered
1 c. fresh blueberries
1 c. fresh blackberries
1 c. fresh raspberries
1 t. sugar, or to taste

Combine all berries in a bowl. Sprinkle with sugar; mix gently.

A large clear glass bowl is a must for entertaining family & friends. Serve up a layered salad, a pasta dish or a sweet dessert trifle...even fill it with water and floating candles to serve as a pretty centerpiece.

7-Fruit Summer Salad

Serves 8 to 10

1/2 c. lime juice
1/2 c. water
1/2 c. sugar
2 nectarines, peeled, pitted and thinly sliced
1 banana, thinly sliced
1 pt. blueberries
1 pt. strawberries, hulled and sliced
1-1/2 c. watermelon, scooped into balls
1-1/2 c. seedless green grapes
1 kiwi, peeled and chopped

Whisk together lime juice, water and sugar in a bowl until sugar is dissolved. Add nectarines and banana; stir to coat and set aside. Combine remaining fruits in a large glass serving bowl. Add nectarine mixture; gently toss to mix. Cover and refrigerate one hour before serving.

Spoon fruit or veggie salads into mini Mason jars...fun for a summer buffet and convenient to tuck in a picnic basket.

Piña Colada Fruit Salad

Makes 4 servings

1/2 c. strawberries, hulled and quartered
1/2 c. blueberries
1/2 c. seedless grapes, halved
1/2 c. pineapple cubes
1 banana, sliced
6-oz. container piña colada yogurt

Combine all fruits in a bowl. Gently stir in yogurt, coating well. Cover and refrigerate for one hour before serving.

Bring back a bit of old-fashioned neighboring...chat across the backyard fence, deliver a warm pie, share a bouquet of sunflowers.

Blueberry-Chicken Salad

Makes 4 servings

2 c. chicken breast, cooked and cubed
3/4 c. celery, chopped
1/2 c. red pepper, diced
1/2 c. green onions, thinly sliced
2 c. blueberries, divided
6-oz. container lemon yogurt
3 T. mayonnaise
1/2 t. salt
Optional: Bibb lettuce

Combine chicken and vegetables in a large bowl. Gently stir in 1-1/2 cups blueberries; reserve remaining berries. Blend remaining ingredients except lettuce. Drizzle over chicken mixture and gently toss to coat. Cover and refrigerate 30 minutes. Spoon onto lettuce-lined plates, if desired. Top with reserved blueberries.

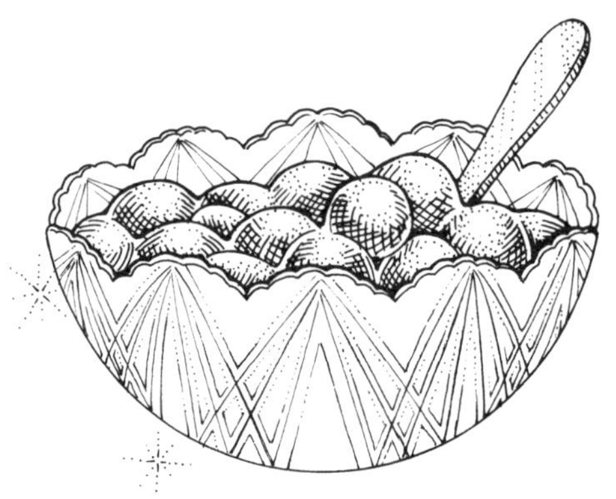

The bright colors of fresh fruit really shine in an antique cut-glass bowl. When washing cut glass, add a little white vinegar to the rinse water...the glass will sparkle!

Marinated Fresh Fruit Salad

Makes 10 servings

2 c. strawberries, hulled and halved or quartered
2 c. seedless green grapes
2 c. seedless red grapes
2 c. blueberries
2 11-oz. cans mandarin oranges, drained
20-oz. can pineapple chunks, drained and 1/4 c. juice reserved

Combine all fruits in a large clear glass serving bowl. Drizzle Marinade over fruit; toss gently to combine. Cover and refrigerate for several hours to overnight. Toss again before serving.

Marinade:

1/4 c. reserved pineapple juice
1/4 c. lemon juice
1/4 c. honey

Whisk together all ingredients in a small bowl.

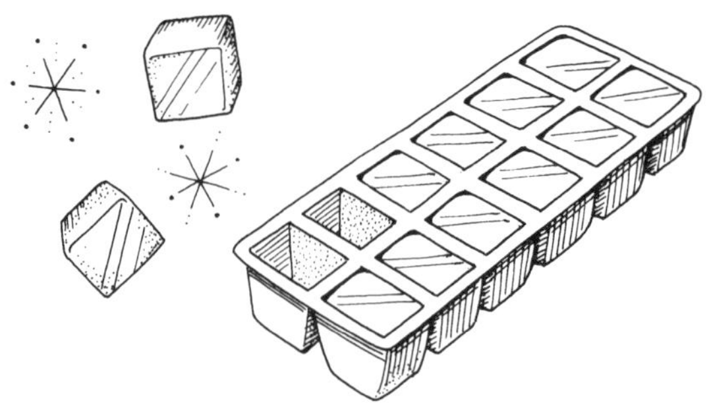

When draining canned fruit, don't toss the juice! Pour it into ice cube trays and freeze...handy for adding a little sweetness to marinades and dressings.

Orzo Fruit Salad

Serves 18 to 20

20-oz. can pineapple chunks, drained and juice reserved
20-oz. can crushed pineapple, drained and juice reserved
2 15-oz. cans mandarin oranges, drained and juice reserved
4-oz. jar maraschino cherries, drained and halved
3/4 c. sugar
2 eggs, beaten
3 T. all-purpose flour
16-oz. pkg. orzo pasta, uncooked
16-oz. container frozen whipped topping, thawed
1 pt. blueberries

In a saucepan over low heat, combine all reserved fruit juices, sugar, eggs and flour. Cook and stir until thickened, about 5 to 10 minutes. Remove from heat; cool for 30 to 60 minutes. Meanwhile, cook pasta according to package directions; drain and rinse with cold water. In a large bowl, combine cooked pasta, pineapple, oranges and cherries to pasta; mix gently. Pour cooled sauce over fruit mixture and toss to coat. Cover and refrigerate until flavors blend, 8 hours or overnight. At serving time, fold in whipped topping and blueberries.

A big, home-baked cookie makes a sweet after-dinner treat. Place each in a cellophane bag tied closed with a ribbon. Family & friends will feel extra special!

Blueberry Linzer Tarts

Makes one dozen

1-1/4 c. butter, softened
2/3 c. sugar
1-1/2 c. almonds, ground
1/8 t. cinnamon
2 c. all-purpose flour
6 T. blueberry preserves
Garnish: powdered sugar

In a bowl, blend butter and sugar until light and fluffy. Stir in almonds, cinnamon and flour, 1/2 cup at a time. Cover and refrigerate for about one hour. On a floured surface, roll out dough 1/8-inch thick. Cut out 24 circles with a 2-1/2 inch round cookie cutter. Cut out the centers of 12 circles with a 1/2-inch mini cookie cutter; leave the remaining 12 circles uncut. Arrange on ungreased baking sheets, one inch apart. Bake at 325 degrees for 10 to 12 minutes, until golden. Cool completely on wire racks. Thinly spread preserves over uncut circles; top with cut-out cookies. Spoon remaining jam into cut-outs; sprinkle with powdered sugar.

Baking bar cookies a few days in advance? They'll stay fresh in their baking pan if tightly covered with aluminum foil.

Blueberry Walnut Squares

Makes 12 to 16 servings

15-1/4 oz. pkg. white cake mix
6 T. all-purpose flour
1-1/4 c. rolled oats, uncooked and divided
1/2 c. butter, softened and divided
1 egg, beaten
21-oz. can blueberry pie filling
1/2 c. chopped walnuts
1/4 c. brown sugar, packed

In a large bowl, combine dry cake mix, flour, one cup oats and 6 tablespoons butter. Mix until crumbly; reserve one cup mixture for topping. To remaining mixture, add egg; mix until well blended. Mixture will be stiff. Press into a greased 13"x9" baking pan. Spoon pie filling over mixture in pan; spread to cover. To reserved crumbs, add remaining oats, remaining butter, walnuts and brown sugar. Mix well; sprinkle over pie filling. Bake at 350 degrees for 35 to 45 minutes, until bubbly and golden.

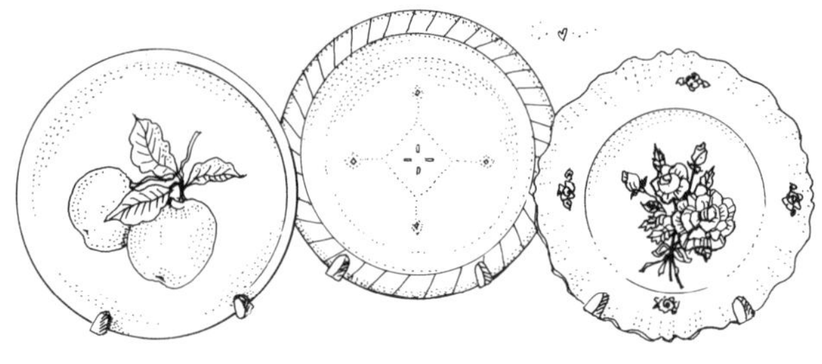

Watch for unusual plates at yard sales. They're just the thing for delivering cookies to friends & neighbors...the recipient will feel extra-special and the dish is theirs to keep.

Blueberry Oatmeal Cookies

Makes 2 dozen

1/2 c. butter
1 c. brown sugar, packed
1 egg, beaten
1 t. vanilla extract
1-1/2 c. old-fashioned oats, uncooked
1 c. all-purpose flour
1/4 t. baking powder
1/2 t. baking soda
1 t. cinnamon
1 t. nutmeg
1 c. frozen blueberries

In a large bowl, blend butter and sugar well. Stir in egg and vanilla; set aside. In a separate bowl, mix oats, flour, baking powder, baking soda and spices; add to butter mixture and mix well. Stir in frozen blueberries; don't worry if some berries break. Drop batter by teaspoonfuls onto ungreased baking sheets. Bake at 350 degrees for 12 to 14 minutes, until golden.

Repurpose a pretty saucer without a teacup as a spoon rest.

Blueberry Drop Cookies

Makes 5 dozen

3/4 c. butter, softened
1 c. sugar
1-1/2 t. lemon zest
2 eggs
2 c. all-purpose flour
2 t. baking powder
1/4 t. salt
Optional: cinnamon to taste
1/2 c. milk
1 c. blueberries

In a large bowl, blend together butter, sugar and zest. Add eggs, one at a time, beating well. In a separate bowl, combine flour, baking powder, salt and cinnamon, if desired. Add flour mixture to butter mixture alternately with milk, beating until smooth. Fold in blueberries. Drop by teaspoonfuls onto greased baking sheets. Bake at 375 degrees for 10 to 12 minutes.

Come along inside...we'll see if tea and buns
can make the world a better place.

-Kenneth Grahame

Super Berry Crisp

Serves 8

21-oz. can cherry pie filling
2 c. fresh blueberries
1/4 c. butter
1/3 c. long-cooking oats, uncooked
1/3 c. all-purpose flour
1/4 c. brown sugar, packed
1 t. sugar
1/4 t. cinnamon
Garnish: whipped cream

Pour pie filling into an ungreased 9" pie plate; fold in blueberries. Melt butter in a small saucepan over medium-low heat. Add remaining ingredients except garnish to melted butter, stirring to coat well. Spread oat mixture over fruit in pie plate. Bake at 350 degrees for 35 minutes, or until topping is crisp and golden. Garnish individual servings with whipped cream.

Top off your best desserts with fresh whipped cream. With an electric mixer on high speed, beat one cup heavy cream until soft peaks form. Add one tablespoon sugar and one teaspoon vanilla extract, then continue to beat until stiff peaks form. Scrumptious!

Peach-Blueberry Crisp

Serves 8

8 peaches, peeled, pitted and sliced
1 c. fresh blueberries
1 T. lemon juice
1/4 c. all-purpose flour
1/3 c. brown sugar, packed
2 T. sugar
1/2 t. vanilla extract

Combine all ingredients in a large bowl; toss lightly. Spoon mixture into an ungreased 9" deep-dish pie plate. Add Topping, breaking it up as you put it on. Bake at 350 degrees for 20 to 25 minutes, until topping is golden.

Topping:

1-1/4 c. all-purpose flour
1/2 c. rolled oats, uncooked
1/2 c. brown sugar, packed
1/2 c. sugar
1/2 c. plus 2 T. butter, melted

Mix all ingredients until crumbly.

Offer mini portions of rich cobblers and crisps. Guests can take "just a taste" of something sweet after a big dinner, or sample several yummy treats.

Fresh Peach-Blueberry Cobbler

Serves 8 to 10

1/2 c. butter, melted
4 c. peaches, peeled, pitted and sliced
1 c. blueberries
2 c. sugar, divided
1-1/4 c. all-purpose flour
2 t. baking powder
1 c. milk
1 t. almond extract
Garnish: vanilla ice cream

Spread melted butter in a 13"x9" baking pan; set aside. Combine peaches and blueberries in a large bowl; add one cup sugar and stir gently to coat evenly. In a separate bowl, mix together remaining sugar, flour, baking powder, milk and extract. Pour into pan; do not stir. Spread fruit mixture evenly over batter. Bake at 375 degrees for 40 to 45 minutes. Fruit will sink into the batter. Serve warm, topped with a scoop of ice cream.

Quickly soften ice cream in the carton using the microwave on high setting...

one pint = 10 to 15 seconds
one quart = 15 to 25 seconds
1/2 gallon = 30 to 40 seconds

Shiny-Top Blueberry Cobbler

Serves 10 to 12

5 to 6 c. fresh blueberries
1-1/2 T. lemon juice
2 c. all-purpose flour
2 c. sugar, divided
2 t. baking powder
1 t. salt, divided
1 c. milk
1/3 c. butter, diced
2 T. cornstarch
1-1/2 c. boiling water
Garnish: vanilla ice cream

Spread berries in a greased shallow 2-1/2 quart casserole dish. Sprinkle with lemon juice; set aside. In a bowl, combine flour, one cup sugar, baking powder, 1/2 teaspoon salt, milk and butter. Stir until well blended. Spoon batter over berries, spreading to edge of dish; set aside. In a small bowl, mix remaining sugar and salt with cornstarch. Sprinkle over batter. Pour boiling water over all; do not stir. Bake at 350 degrees for one hour, or until bubbly, golden and glazed. Serve warm or cooled, topped with ice cream.

The diner is everybody's kitchen.

-Richard Gutman

New England Blueberry Coffee Cake *Makes 12 servings*

1-1/2 c. all-purpose flour
1/2 c. sugar
1 T. baking powder
1 t. cinnamon
1/2 t. salt
1-1/2 c. blueberries
1 egg
1/2 c. milk
1/4 c. butter, melted

Combine dry ingredients together; gently fold in blueberries and set aside. Whisk egg, milk and butter together in a small mixing bowl; add to flour mixture, stirring carefully. Pour into a greased 8"x8" baking pan; sprinkle with Topping. Bake at 425 degrees for 20 to 25 minutes.

Topping:

1/4 c. butter, melted
3/4 c. brown sugar, packed
1 T. all-purpose flour
Optional: 1/2 c. chopped walnuts

Combine ingredients; mix well.

Try steel-cut oats in recipes that call for regular long-cooking oats. Steel-cut oats are less processed, for a pleasing chewy texture you're sure to enjoy.

Blueberry & Caramel Coffee Cake

Serves 6 to 8

16.3-oz. tube refrigerated jumbo biscuits
1/2 c. brown sugar, packed
3 T. butter, melted
3/4 t. cinnamon
3/4 c. quick-cooking oats, uncooked and divided
1-1/2 c. fresh or frozen blueberries
1/4 c. sugar
2 T. butter, diced

Separate biscuits; cut into 4 to 8 pieces each. In a generously greased 11"x8" baking pan, arrange biscuit pieces in a single layer as much as possible. Set aside. In a small bowl, combine brown sugar, melted butter and cinnamon. Spoon over biscuits; sprinkle with 1/2 cup oats. In another bowl, combine blueberries and sugar; toss until coated evenly. Spoon over oats and biscuits. Sprinkle with remaining oats; dot with butter. Bake, uncovered, at 375 degrees for about 25 to 30 minutes, until golden. Serve warm. Best reheated in oven, not microwave.

Keep an eye open for those great milk pitchers like Grandma used to have. Shaped like a rooster or cow, they add a spark of whimsy to any breakfast or dessert table.

Very Blueberry Coffee Cake

Makes 8 to 10 servings

1/2 c. butter, room temperature
1 c. sugar
2 eggs, room temperature
1-1/2 t. vanilla extract
8-oz. container sour cream
3 c. all-purpose flour
2 t. baking powder
1/2 t. baking soda
1/2 t. salt
2 c. fresh blueberries, divided
1/4 c. coarse sugar

Combine butter and sugar in a large bowl. Using an electric mixer fitted with a paddle attachment, beat on medium-high speed until light and fluffy, about 5 minutes. Turn mixer to low speed; beat in eggs, one at a time. Beat in vanilla and sour cream. In a separate bowl, sift together flour, baking powder, baking soda and salt. Add flour mixture to batter; beat on low speed until just mixed. Do not overmix. Fold in 1-1/2 cups blueberries with a spatula, mixing gently. Spoon batter into a 9"x9" baking pan coated with non-stick vegetable spray. Scatter remaining berries over the top; press in lightly and sprinkle with coarse sugar. Bake at 350 degrees for 35 to 40 minutes, until lightly golden and a toothpick comes out clean.

Once in a young lifetime, one should be allowed to have as much sweetness as one can possibly want and hold.

-Judith Olney

Wild Blueberry Gingerbread

Makes 13 to 15 servings

2-1/2 c. all-purpose flour
1 c. sugar
1/2 t. ground cloves
1/2 t. cinnamon
1/2 t. ground ginger
1 t. salt
1 t. baking soda
1/2 c. molasses
2 eggs, beaten
1/2 c. oil
1 c. hot tea
1 c. fresh blueberries
Garnish: whipped cream

In a large bowl, mix together flour, sugar, spices and baking soda. Stir in molasses, eggs, oil and tea. Carefully fold in blueberries. Spoon batter into a greased and floured 13"x9" baking pan. Bake at 350 degrees for about 35 minutes, until a toothpick inserted in the center tests clean. Cool; cut into squares and top with a dollop of whipped cream.

Grease and flour cake pans in one easy step! Combine 1/2 cup shortening with 1/4 cup all-purpose flour. Keep this handy mix in a covered jar stored at room temperature.

Blueberry-Citrus Cake

Serves 10 to 12

15-1/4 oz. pkg. lemon cake mix
6 T. all-purpose flour
1 c. water
1/2 c. plus 2 T. orange juice, divided
1/3 c. oil
3 eggs, beaten
1-1/2 c. fresh or frozen blueberries
1 T. orange zest
1 T. lemon zest
1 c. powdered sugar
Garnish: additional orange and lemon zests

Beat cake mix, flour, water, 1/2 cup orange juice, oil and eggs in a large bowl with an electric mixer at low speed for 30 seconds. Increase speed to medium; beat for 2 minutes. With a wooden spoon, gently fold in blueberries and zests. Pour batter into a greased and floured Bundt® pan. Bake at 350 degrees for 35 to 40 minutes, until a toothpick inserted in center comes out clean. Cool completely in pan on a wire rack. Remove from pan. Blend remaining orange juice and powdered sugar until smooth; drizzle over cake. Garnish with zests.

Before adding raisins, nuts, dried or fresh fruit to cake batter, toss them with a little flour...it keeps them from sinking to the bottom of the cake.

Shrewsberry Cake

Makes 12 to 15 servings

1 c. butter, softened
3 c. sugar
3 eggs
3 c. all-purpose flour
1 t. baking powder
1 c. milk
1/2 c. applesauce
2 t. vanilla extract
2 c. fresh blueberries

In a large bowl, beat butter and sugar with an electric mixer on medium speed. Add eggs, one at a time, beating for 3 to 5 minutes after each egg. Add remaining ingredients except blueberries and beat well. Fold in blueberries. Transfer batter to a greased and sugared tube pan. Bake at 350 degrees for one hour and 15 minutes. Cool cake in pan for 15 minutes before removing.

Diners are famous for oh-so perfect pie crust. Their secret is using equal amounts of chilled butter and room-temperature shortening for a tender & flaky pastry every time!

Berry Delicious Pie

Makes 8 servings

3/4 c. sugar
3 T. cornstarch
1/8 t. salt
1/4 c. water
5 c. blueberries, divided
1 T. butter
1 T. lemon juice
9-inch pie crust, baked
Garnish: whipped topping

Heat sugar, cornstarch, salt and water in a saucepan until sugar dissolves, stirring until smooth. Add 3 cups blueberries; bring to a boil for 2 minutes, stirring constantly or until thickened and bubbly. Remove from heat; add butter, lemon juice and remaining blueberries. Stir until butter is melted; cool. Pour blueberry mixture into pie crust; refrigerate until serving. Serve with a dollop of whipped topping.

Try sugar substitutes made especially for baking to turn out sweet, golden, moist goodies with half the sugar. There's even a brown sugar variety! Be sure to check the package for how to measure correctly.

Red, White & Blue Pie

Makes 8 servings

9-inch pie crust, baked
2 c. fresh blueberries
2 c. fresh or frozen red raspberries
1 c. sugar
3 T. cornstarch
1/4 t. salt
1/4 c. water
1 t. butter
Optional: whipped cream

Fill pie crust with blueberries; set aside. In a saucepan over medium heat, combine raspberries, sugar, cornstarch, salt and water. Cook until thickened and well blended, stirring often. Stir in butter; cool slightly. Spoon over blueberries in pie crust. Cover and chill. Serve topped with whipped cream, if desired.

To keep a chilled dessert cool on a warm day, just fill a picnic basket with plastic zipping bags full of ice, lay a colorful tea towel over the ice and set the sweets on top.

Blueberry Cream Pie

Serves 6 to 8

8-oz. container sour cream
2 T. all-purpose flour
3/4 c. sugar
1 t. vanilla extract
1/4 t. salt
1 egg, beaten
2-1/2 c. fresh blueberries
9-inch pie crust, unbaked

In a bowl, combine all ingredients except blueberries and crust. Beat with an electric mixer on high speed until well mixed, about 2 minutes. Fold in blueberries; pour into unbaked pie crust. Bake at 400 degrees for 25 minutes; remove from oven. Sprinkle pie with Topping; bake an additional 10 minutes. Chill before serving.

Topping:

3 T. all-purpose flour
1 T. sugar
1-1/2 t. butter
3 T. chopped pecans or walnuts

Stir ingredients together until crumbly.

If dessert is a flop, layer it with whipped cream in a parfait glass and give it a fancy name. Nobody will know the difference!

Berry Patch Slab Pie

Makes 24 servings

14.1-oz. pkg. refrigerated pie crusts
2 8-oz. pkgs. cream cheese, softened
2/3 c. sugar
1 T. milk
3 c. strawberries, hulled and sliced
3 c. blueberries
1 c. strawberry glaze

Soften pie crusts as directed on package. On a lightly floured surface, unroll crusts and stack one on top of the other. Roll out to a 17-inch by 12-inch rectangle. Fit doubled crust into an ungreased 15"x10" jelly-roll pan, pressing crust into corners of pan. Crimp edges of crust; pierce crust all over with a fork. Bake at 350 degrees for 10 to 12 minutes, until golden. Set on a wire rack to cool completely, about 30 minutes. In a bowl, blend cream cheese, sugar and milk until smooth. Spread mixture onto cooled crust with a spatula. Chill for about one hour, until set. In a large bowl, combine all berries and glaze; mix gently. Spoon berry mixture over cream cheese. Cover and refrigerate until serving time. Cut into squares.

For best results when baking, allow butter and eggs to come to room temperature. Just set them out on the counter about an hour ahead of time and they'll be ready.

Fresh Blueberry Pie

Serves 6 to 8

3/4 c. sugar
3 T. cornstarch
1/8 t. salt
1/2 t. cinnamon
4 c. blueberries
2 9-inch pie crusts
1 T. lemon juice
2 T. butter

Combine sugar, cornstarch, salt and cinnamon in a small bowl; sprinkle over blueberries. Line a 9" pie plate with one crust; pour berry mixture inside. Sprinkle with lemon juice and dot with butter. Roll out remaining pie crust to fit the top; crimp and flute edges. Vent top. Bake at 425 degrees for 30 to 40 minutes or until crust is golden.

Write it on your heart that every day is
the best day of the year.

-Ralph Waldo Emerson

Blueberries & Cream Pull-Aparts

Makes about 15 servings per pan

1 T. active dry yeast
2 c. milk, scalded
1/3 c. oil
1 t. salt
1/3 c. sugar
5 to 6 c. all-purpose flour
2 eggs, beaten
1 c. butter, melted and divided
3-1/2 oz. box instant vanilla pudding mix
1 c. blueberries

Let yeast sit in cooled scalded milk for 10 minutes; mix with oil, salt, sugar, flour and eggs. Allow dough to double in bulk; roll out on a lightly floured surface to 1/2-inch thickness. Cut dough with a biscuit cutter or round glass into about 30 rounds. Pour 1/2 cup butter into each of two Bundt® pans; dip rounds in butter then in vanilla pudding mix. Line sides and bottom of pans with rounds, overlapping edges, using 15 per pan. Sprinkle blueberries between rounds; bake at 400 degrees for 20 minutes.

Keep a cherished cookbook clean and free of spatters. Slip it into a gallon-size plastic zipping bag before cooking up a favorite recipe.

Blueberry Dream Dessert

Serves 6 to 8

2 c. rolled oats, uncooked
1 c. plus 1 T. all-purpose flour, divided
1 c. brown sugar, packed
3/4 c. butter, melted
2 c. fresh blueberries
3/4 c. grape juice or water
1/2 c. sugar
2 T. lemon juice
1/8 t. salt
Garnish: vanilla ice cream or whipped cream

In a bowl, combine oats, one cup flour and brown sugar. Add melted butter and mix well until crumbly; set aside 1/2 cup of crumb mixture for topping. Press remaining mixture into the bottom of a lightly greased 8"x8" baking pan. In a saucepan over medium heat, combine blueberries, remaining flour, grape juice or water, sugar, lemon juice and salt. Simmer for about 5 minutes. Remove from heat. Allow to cool for several minutes; pour over crust in pan. Sprinkle with reserved crumb mixture. Bake at 350 degrees for 45 minutes. Garnish as desired.

Save time when baking...tuck measuring cups into your countertop canisters. They'll be ready to scoop out flour and sugar when you need them.

Summer Blueberry Buckle

Makes 4 to 6 servings

1/4 c. butter, softened
3/4 c. sugar
1 egg, beaten
2 c. all-purpose flour
2 t. baking powder
1/2 t. salt
1/2 c. milk
2 c. fresh or frozen blueberries, thawed

In a bowl, blend butter and sugar; add egg and beat well. In a separate bowl, sift together flour, baking powder and salt. Stir milk into butter mixture alternately with flour mixture. Gently fold in blueberries; spread batter evenly in a buttered 9"x9" baking pan. Sprinkle with Topping. Bake at 350 degrees for 35 to 40 minutes.

Topping:

1/4 c. butter, softened
1/2 c. sugar
1/3 c. all-purpose flour
1/2 t. cinnamon

Blend all ingredients together.

Make dessert a grand finale...serve it on your prettiest china plates!

Heavenly Angel Dessert

Serves 12

8-oz. pkg. cream cheese, softened
1 c. powdered sugar
8-oz. container frozen whipped topping, thawed
14-oz. bakery angel food cake, cut into 1-inch cubes
1 to 2 21-oz. cans blueberry pie filling

In a large bowl, beat together cream cheese and powdered sugar. Fold in whipped topping and cake cubes; spread evenly into a 13"x9" baking pan. Top with pie filling. Cover and refrigerate for at least 2 hours or overnight. Cut into squares.

Fresh-picked berries are a special country pleasure. Store them in a colander in the refrigerator to let cold air circulate around them. Wash them when you're ready to use them.

Aunt Marge's Special Blueberry Dessert

Serves 6

2 c. blueberries
3 T. lemon juice
3 T. butter, softened
1-1/2 c. sugar, divided
1/4 t. salt
1 c. all-purpose flour
1 t. baking powder
1/2 c. milk
Optional: 1/2 t. cinnamon
1 T. cornstarch
1 c. boiling water

Place blueberries in a lightly greased 9"x9" baking pan; drizzle with lemon juice and set aside. In a large bowl, blend together butter, 3/4 cup sugar and salt; set aside. In a separate bowl, mix together flour and baking powder. Add flour mixture and milk alternately to butter mixture; stir well. Pour batter over blueberries; sprinkle with cinnamon, if desired. In a small bowl, combine cornstarch and remaining sugar; sprinkle over top. Pour boiling water over top. Bake at 350 degrees for 45 minutes, or until golden on top.

Take Mom or Grandma along to a farmstand and ask her to share her tried & true fruity dessert recipes with you. You may find a new favorite or two!

Angel Berry Dessert

Makes 8 to 10 servings

1 baked angel food cake
3 c. frozen blueberries, raspberries and/or strawberries, thawed and juice reserved
1 c. sugar
1 c. water
6-oz. pkg. strawberry gelatin mix

In a large clear glass bowl, break cake into bite-size pieces; set aside. In a separate bowl, combine thawed berries, reserved juice and sugar. Stir until sugar is dissolved and set aside. Bring water to a boil in a small saucepan; add gelatin mix and stir well to dissolve. Pour gelatin over cake pieces. Allow to soak into the cake for several minutes; do not stir. Gently fold berry mixture into cake mixture. Cover and refrigerate until set. Serve chilled.

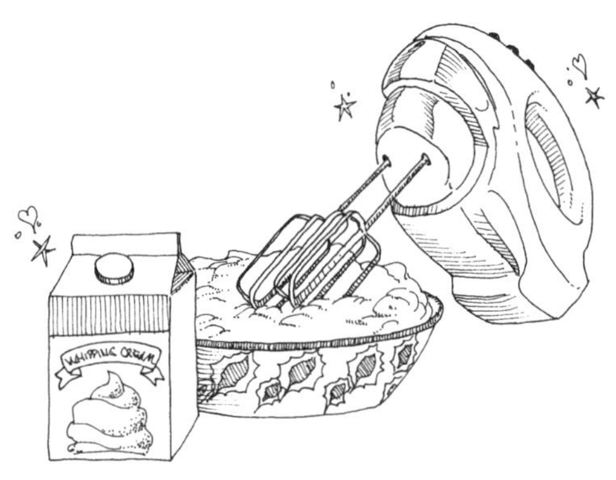

Grandma's best old-fashioned fruit desserts are always delicious with fresh whipped cream. Beat a cup of whipping cream until soft peaks form. Mix in 2 teaspoons sugar and 2 teaspoons vanilla extract...and enjoy!

Grandma's Spiced Blueberry Grunt

Makes 4 to 6 servings

1 c. water
1 c. sugar
1/2 t. cinnamon
4 c. blueberries
Optional: 1 t. lemon juice

Make Dough Topping; set aside. In a large saucepan over medium heat, combine water, sugar and cinnamon; stir in blueberries. If berries aren't very tart, stir in lemon juice. Bring to a light boil while stirring gently. Drop Dough Topping over blueberry mixture by large spoonfuls. Cover and cook over low heat for 12 to 15 minutes, until dough is done. Serve warm.

Dough Topping:

2 c. all-purpose flour
2 t. baking powder
1/2 t. baking soda
1/2 t. salt
1/4 c. butter
1 c. buttermilk

Mix together flour, baking powder, baking soda and salt. Cut in butter with a fork or mix it with your hands. Stir in buttermilk, being careful not to overmix.

Create a fun centerpiece for an ice cream social. Clean an empty ice cream container (or ask the local store for extras), fill with floral foam and tuck in some bright flowers.

Blueberry Cheesecake Punch Bowl Trifle

Makes 10 servings

1 angel food cake, cubed
2 8-oz. pkgs. cream cheese, room temperature
3/4 c. whipping cream
1/2 c. sour cream
1 t. vanilla extract
1 c. powdered sugar
21-oz. can blueberry pie filling, divided

Add cake cubes to a punch bowl; set aside. In another bowl, combine remaining ingredients except pie filling; beat with an electric mixer on medium speed until smooth and creamy. Spoon half of cream cheese mixture over cake; dollop with half of pie filling. Repeat layers. Cover and chill until serving time.

APPETIZERS & SNACKS

BEVERAGES

BREADS

BREAKFAST

CAKES

COOKIES & BARS

Our Story

Back in 1984, we were next-door neighbors raising our families in the little town of Delaware, Ohio. Two moms with small children, we were looking for a way to do what we loved and stay home with the kids too. We had always shared a love of home cooking and making memories with family & friends and so, after many a conversation over the backyard fence, **Gooseberry Patch** was born.

We put together our first catalog at our kitchen tables, enlisting the help of our loved ones wherever we could. From that very first mailing, we found an immediate connection with many of our customers and it wasn't long before we began receiving letters, photos and recipes from these new friends. In 1992, we put together our very first cookbook, compiled from hundreds of these recipes and, the rest, as they say, is history.

Hard to believe it's been over 40 years since those kitchen-table days! From that original little **Gooseberry Patch** family, we've grown to include an amazing group of creative folks who love cooking, decorating and creating as much as we do. Today, we're best known for our homestyle, family-friendly cookbooks, now recognized as national bestsellers.

One thing's for sure, we couldn't have done it without our friends all across the country. Each year, we're honored to turn thousands of your recipes into our collectible cookbooks. Our hope is that each book captures the stories and heart of all of you who have shared with us. Whether you've been with us since the beginning or are just discovering us, welcome to the **Gooseberry Patch** family!

Jo Ann & Vickie

Visit our website anytime

www.gooseberrypatch.com

1·800·854·6673